The Wisest Coin in the City of Sand

A Pocket Parable of Prosperity by E.P. Willow

THE WISEST COIN IN THE CITY OF SAND

First edition. August 10, 2025.

ISBN: 979-8231301522

Written by E.P. Willow.

A single coin saved is not the end of wealth, but the seed of it.

Guard it, grow it, and in time, it will teach you more than gold ever could.

Dedication

To the quiet earners, the patient builders, and the ones who keep going-

May your wisdom shine brighter than gold.

Introduction

Welcome, reader.

This is not a book of formulas. It is a book of

principles told through parables inspired by the wisdom of old and the hustle of today.

Each story you read is a reflection of timeless truths: that wealth is built slowly, silently, and with intention.

Take your time. Reread the scrolls. And most importantly, act on them.

- E.P. Willow

Chapter 1:
The Man Who Saved One Coin

In the city of Sand, where the winds whispered through the alleys of ancient stone, lived a man named Kael.

A potter by trade, Kael earned modest coin shaping clay into bowls, jars, and flasks. The market was often unkind, and customers were scarce. Yet despite meager earnings, Kael made a vow: every day, he would save one coin.

His neighbors scoffed. "One coin? What can that do?" But Kael only smiled and placed the coin into a cloth pouch hidden beneath his floor.

Months passed, and Kael's pouch grew heavier. Not just in weight, but in meaning. Each coin symbolized his discipline, his belief in tomorrow. One evening, after a long day, his apprentice asked him, "Master, why do you save so when others spend freely?"

Kael replied, "A coin kept is a slave that earns. A coin spent is a soldier that dies. My army is growing."

Years later, Kael's pouch became a fund used to purchase a better kiln, followed by a second stall in the market. The man who once saved one coin a day became the man whose coins served him.

Wisdom Scroll:

- Keep at least 1/10 of all you earn

- Let your savings work for you before you work for others

- The smallest coin, saved daily, becomes a fortune yearly

Chapter 2: The Law of Empty Purses

Jorah was the best baker in the Northern Quarter. His breads were warm, soft, and sold out each day before noon.

And yet, by nightfall, his purse lay empty.

His friends envied his trade, assuming he lived like a king. But Jorah had no riches-only regrets. One night, a beggar offered to sweep his shop in exchange for stale crusts. Jorah obliged. As they talked, the beggar asked, "How is it that you work more than most, yet remain poor?" Jorah sighed, "My earnings vanish like mist."

The beggar nodded, "The purse that eats all it earns shall always be hungry. Feed it less."

That night, Jorah sat by candlelight, writing every coin earned and every coin spent. For the first time, he saw the leaks-the luxuries, the indulgences, the forgotten

tips.

The next morning, he changed. He brought a smaller coin pouch to market and vowed never to spend from his earnings until he'd set aside his portion to keep.

Months later, Jorah not only had savings but peace.

Wisdom Scroll:

- Spend less than you earn

- Wealth begins with awareness and discipline
- Track your gold, lest it slip away unseen

Chapter 3: Ten Truths from a Tired Merchant

Karek had sailed the Salt Sea twenty-seven times and traded in twelve cities. Now old and stooped, he no longer sought riches, but the company of the young. Ten apprentices gathered to hear his final teachings before he hung up his merchant's sash for good.

He stood beneath a fig tree in the center of the square and said, "Each of you shall receive not coin nor land from me-but truths.

These are the ten truths that bought me ships, lost me fortunes, and returned me peace."

He handed each apprentice a scroll. "Read aloud," he commanded.

They read, one after the other:

1. Wealth is first a habit, then a result.
2. Delay desire; earn before you enjoy.
3. Not all risks are worthy.
4. Ask the wise before investing.
5. A humble home fills faster than a vast palace.
6. Do not lend what you cannot lose.
7. Gold runs from the ungrateful.
8. Knowledge weighs nothing but is richer than rubies.
9. Record what you earn, or it will escape.
10. Every day spent learning makes your purse heavier.

They asked, "Which truth made you the richest?"

Karek said, "Number nine. I knew what I had and what I lost. And thus I knew what I needed."

The apprentices bowed low, not for the gold, but for the grit of wisdom earned over years of tides.

Wisdom Scroll:

- Riches grow in record books before they grow in vaults

- Do not confuse boldness with blindness

- You are as wealthy as the wisdom you retain

Chapter 4: The Gold That Grew Wings

Mira's fingers wove silk into wonders, and yet her coin purse was always thin. When her friend Elan approached her with a grand idea-a traveling marketplace with profits for all, she gave him every coin she had saved.

"It will double in a month," he promised.

A month passed. Then two. Elan disappeared.

Mira wept-not for the coins, but for her broken trust. Her grandfather came to her home and listened. Then he said, "Gold in the wrong hands grows wings and flies."

Mira sat beside him, pen and paper in hand. She asked him how he had kept wealth through wars, storms, and betrayal.

"Gold must be courted like a lover," he said. "Trusted to those who protect, not charm. Before you invest, ask:

Does the person protect their own coin? Do they understand the weight of losing yours?"

Mira spent the next year learning. Not weaving-learning. By year's end, she knew more about trade, market patterns, and risk than most men twice her age. She invested again-but not with Elan.

Her new coins did not fly. They marched in rows and multiplied.

Wisdom Scroll:

- Investigate before you invest

- Hope is a good dream, but a bad plan

- Gold stays where it is respected and studied

Chapter 5: The Scribe's Secret Scroll

In the back of the city's grand archive, behind shelves untouched for decades, sat an old scribe named Tavon. He had copied thousands of scrolls, yet never owned a purse with more than a few coins. One stormy evening, a traveler named Lin asked Tavon if he had read anything useful in all those years of writing.

The scribe chuckled and gestured to a sealed drawer. Inside was a single parchment titled: 'The Scroll of Self-Created Wealth'.

"Why hide it?" Lin asked.

"Because most want gold without effort. This scroll speaks only to the disciplined."

The scroll read

'You are not poor if you know how to create value. Learn what others ignore.

Offer what others need. Trade what others desire.'

Tavon had used the scroll's wisdom not to gather wealth, but to give advice to those ready to receive it. Five of the city's wealthiest merchants had once sat at his desk as paupers, reading that scroll.

Lin read it again and asked, "What does it mean to create value?"

"Solve pain," Tavon replied. "Every coin ever earned began with a pain eased."

Lin left with no coins in hand. But within a year, he returned wealthy. Not because he found treasure, but because he solved a problem with the skill he honed.

Wisdom Scroll:

- Learn a skill no one can take from you

- Every fortune is built on solving problems

- A wise scroll read once teaches little, a wise scroll read often builds wealth

Chapter 6: The Basketmaker's Covenant

Toma's hands wove baskets so fine, they seemed fit for royalty. Yet few bought them. Day after day, he sat in the market, smiling at passersby who offered only compliments, not coins.

Frustrated, he considered giving up. But one night, an old traveler suggested something strange: "Give your baskets away for a week."

"Give?" Toma echoed.

"Yes. Give them to the ten kindest strangers. Ask for nothing. Give with joy."

Toma hesitated, then obeyed.

On the first day, a woman wept upon receiving a basket. She used it to carry her goods to the healer. On the third day, a merchant used it to display fruits, and others asked where he got it. By the end of the week, ten baskets had reached ten homes, and word of their beauty had spread farther than coin ever had.

The following week, Toma sold more than he ever had. Soon, he couldn't keep up with orders.

"A covenant of giving," he said, "was the seed of my abundance."

Wisdom Scroll:

- Generosity precedes prosperity

- Reputation is the silent salesman

- To be remembered, give more than expected

Chapter 7:
Five Stones of Fortune

When Kael grew old, he passed his pouch to his daughter. But before doing so, he placed five small stones inside, each painted with a single word:

Learn, Save, Guard, Multiply, Teach. She asked, "What are these, Father?"

"The five stones of fortune," he said. "Each one must be held in your hand and heart."

He explained:

- Learn: Find wisdom before chasing gold. Study those who have done what you hope to do.

- Save: Keep a part of all you earn. Even when the winds are against you.

- Guard: Do not throw your coins to fools. Protect your earnings like your life.

- Multiply: Make your money work while you sleep

- Teach: Pass the knowledge, or the treasure will be buried with you.

The daughter carried those stones everywhere. She built a business selling clothes across the provinces. Every new worker received their own set of painted stones.

Years later, when she died, hundreds gathered not because of her wealth, but because of what she had taught them.

Wisdom Scroll:

- Wisdom multiplies when shared

- The richest inheritances are not gold, but guidance

- Fortune follows those who follow principles

Chapter 8:
The Artist and the Empty Jar

Lani was a painter whose works could stir hearts, yet her pockets were always empty. She painted with passion but lacked discipline.

At every festival, she sold a few pieces, then spent the coin on food, trinkets, or fleeting pleasures.

One evening, her mentor visited and gifted her a small clay jar.

"What is this?" she asked.

"Your proof of patience," he said. "After every sale, place one coin in this jar. Seal it. Do not touch it until the jar is full."

Reluctantly, Lani obeyed. She began dropping a single coin in the jar after each sale. At first, it felt small, meaningless. But as the clinking sound grew louder with time, so did her sense of pride. She painted more, sold more, and spent less.

Months later, when the jar was full, she broke it open to find a small fortune. She reinvested it into better brushes, canvas, and a solo exhibit.

Her reputation flourished.

"Even beauty must learn discipline," she said, standing beside her paintings at her first gallery.

Wisdom Scroll:

- Celebrate income with saving, not spending

- The smallest discipline builds the strongest foundation

- True artists master not only their craft, but their coin

Chapter 9: The Fisherman's Three Nets

Bren rose with the sun each day and cast his nets into the sea. But unlike others, he carried not one net, but three.

A young boy once asked him, "Why three nets?" "One for today," Bren said, casting the first. "One for

the tides-those uncertain days when fish flee." He cast the

second.

"And one for the storm," he added, laying the third net beside him, folded and dry.

When days were good, he saved a portion of fish and dried them for lean times. When storms came and boats remained docked, he still had food and trade.

His neighbors often mocked his caution-until the great storm struck. While others begged and bartered, Bren ate in peace and sold dried fish at a premium.

He later used the profits to buy a second boat and taught the boy how to fish with three nets.

Wisdom Scroll:

- Build more than one stream of income

- Save not only for joy, but for the inevitable storm

- Prepare in calm so you are not broken in a crisis

Chapter 10:
The Stonecutter's Ledger

Derek was known for carving tombstones and temple steps, but quietly, he was also the best ledger keeper in the city.

For every coin earned, he etched the amount into a small leather book. Every copper spent on bread, rope, tools was recorded with the same care he gave to chiseling stone.

His fellow workers laughed at his habit. "You spend more time writing your money than using it!"

But Derek never missed a payment, never ran short, never borrowed in desperation.

When asked how he always seemed stable while others struggled, he showed them his ledger.

"Wealth," he said, "isn't about having much-it's about losing little. And I lose nothing, because I forget nothing."

Wisdom Scroll:

- Write down everything your gold does

- Forgetting is the fastest thief

- Wealth doesn't leak from purses-it leaks from the untracked mind

Chapter 11: The Firewood Seller's Secret

Ari sold firewood from sunrise to sunset. Most saw him as just another laborer. But Ari had a secret.

He worked one hour longer than anyone else, and he saved every coin earned in that final hour.

At first, the extra coins were small. But he never missed a day. After a year, he had enough to buy a sturdier cart. Then, a mule.

Then, a second worker.

After a decade, Ari no longer carried firewood himself-he managed a team of ten, owned a warehouse, and sold not just wood, but tools and lanterns.

When asked his secret, he pointed to the hourglass on his shelf.

"That last hour," he said, "was never for today. It was for the man I hoped to become."

Wisdom Scroll:

- Invest one hour daily in your future

- Small, consistent effort outlasts bursts of luck

- Wealth blooms in the hour no one watches

Chapter 12: The Pebble and the Mountain

A child once approached the elder Kael and asked, "How did you build all this? The shop, the land, the gold?"

Kael handed him a single pebble.

"Move this from here to the far wall," he said. The child did.

"Now imagine doing that each day for a mountain." "But that would take forever!" the child exclaimed. "Not forever," Kael smiled. "Just every day."

Kael explained how he began with one coin, one customer, one habit. And how those habits grew, like pebbles added to a hill.

Eventually, the hill became a monument, and the monument became his legacy.

Wisdom Scroll:

- Wealth is built daily, not instantly
- The first step is never glorious, but always essential
- Begin with a pebble. Move it. Repeat.

Final Reflection

You've read the scrolls. Now write your own.

Begin with one habit. One coin. One disciplined decision. Legacy is not written in stone-it's shaped by daily choices.

Don't miss out!

Visit the website below and you can sign up to receive emails whenever E.P. Willow publishes a new book. There's no charge and no obligation.

https://books2read.com/r/B-A-LQVJE-PLUTG

BOOKS 2 READ

Connecting independent readers to independent writers.

Also by E.P. Willow

The Wisest Coin in the City of Sand

www.ingramcontent.com/pod-product-compliance
Lightning Source LLC
LaVergne TN
LVHW090336210926
848480LV00004B/1443

Jean-Gérard Bursztein

The Unconscious, its Space-Time

Aristotle, Lacan, Poincaré

Translated by Richard Klein

hermann
Depuis 1876

[...] if memory, which is more or less unconscious of these successive positions, is necessary for the genesis of the notion of space, this memory can go back more or less quite far into the past. From this results in the very definition of space a certain indetermination which constitutes its relativity.

Henri Poincaré, *Science et méthode*, éd. Kimé, 1999, p. 94.

Foreword

In this essay I tried to develop the theme *the unconscious, its space-time* that Freud had proposed during the discussion on 8 November 1911 in the context of the Wednesday soirées with his colleagues. I'll quote it:

> In the metapsychological mode of envisaging the phenomena, there exists a system which functions without the element of time. A step that would render this schema more useful would be the following: what we are studying are the processes which are not produced within the psychical systems [...] but between them. [...] On the other hand, this system [intrapsychical] has something which resembles what we call space when we refer to objects.'[1]

It is remarkable that Freud has argued, on the one hand, that the object of the work bears upon the intrapsychic relations and, on the other hand, he emphasised this question of having to be treated through what he designated as *spatiality.*

These questions have remained without a reply since then. One can nevertheless begin a reply using the topological hypotheses of Jacques Lacan concerning the unconscious, which is what I attempt in this essay.

---

1. Freud, S., 'session of 8 November 1911', in *The first psychoanalysts*, Collective, Minutes of the Psychoanalytical Society of Vienna, vol. III: 1910-1911, Knowledge Collection on the Unconscious, Series, Psychoanalysis in its history, Gallimard, 1979, p. 300.

I.

Topology and subjective formalism in psychoanalysis

1.1 Accessibility to structure

In this essay I want to show that formalism and topology are not just abstractions but are above all modes of access to the unconscious, opening up onto a broad legibility of its structure (not for everyone but for those who have acquired by experience of the treatment *a knowledge of the psychoanalyst*). In this epistemological perspective I am opposing *history* to *structure*. I start with Freud who, in his texts of 1938 and in *The Man Moses and Monotheism*,[1] invented a sort of *historical myth* that he called *historical truth*, in order to think the origin of structure. I will come back to the contents of this myth, which repeats the supposition of what he names the *murder of the father*. He postulates that there exists in civilisation this repetition of a murder generating guilt, obliging the filial assassins to bring about the Law of the dead father as the *symbolic Law*, that is to say civilisation.

Today, some analysts are taking up again this notion of historical myth and historical truth by developing an imaginary

1. Freud, S., *Moses and Monotheism*, SE XXIII, Hogarth press and the Institute of Psycho-Analysis, London, 1934-8, and Vintage Books, London, 2001.

theory that gives a proper place to structure, the Freudian theory of the murder of the father as the condition for the invention of civilisation. Opposite to such a procedure, to something so imaginary, I propose not to begin with the supposed genesis of civilisation, but with its existence *always already given* as much for the social bond as for the unconscious. Moreover, having proposed this existence as always already given, my hypothesis will be that the unconscious possesses a spatiality implying a structure that I name after Lacan (R, S, I) (I want to show that only these topological structures, where the unconscious is situated, account for so many of its internal changes as well as for its modes of temporality. This hypothesis allows for the taking up of open problems not resolved by Freud.

1.2 AN EPISTEMOLOGY LINKED TO THE LETTER

I'll use as support Lacan's seminar, *Concerning a discourse which would not be that of the semblant*[2] in which he proposes what he calls the *letter*. He refers to Newton's gesture who, far from abandoning himself to a theological interrogation without end on the nature of the universe, took the decision to no longer make hypotheses on this universe but to reduce the real of the universe to a *play of letters*[3] explaining the laws of its functioning. It's the procedure of Lacanian epistemology. In effect, the latter places at a distance the concrete aspect of his praxis in order to constitute not only a theoretical horizon but also to extend it in the form of a formal horizon which

2. Lacan, J., *Le séminaire, Livre XVIII, D'un discours qui ne serait pas du semblant:1971*, Paris, Seuil, 2006.

3. In 1687, Newton published '*The Mathematical Principles of Natural Philosophy*' in which he exposes the laws of the movement of bodies and the law of universal gravitation, laws asserted since in the form of letters. One expresses Newton's law of gravitation in the form: $F_1 = F_2 = Gm_1 \times m_2/r^2$.

potentially can express in a general way the variations of the unconscious. One sees that to proceed in this way, one obtains a much richer perception of the structure of the unconscious and of the possibilities of its transformations.

1.3 Space as a fundamental epistemological category in psychoanalysis

I am trying to make headway in the problematic of temporality in the unconscious that Freud has barely sketched out. How to grasp the differences in temporality between the time in repetition of unconscious contents – that Freud designated as timeless – and the time for the passage to the conscious? Modalities of temporality under which Freud exerted himself to think what I am calling *structure* and what I take from Lacanian psychoanalysis.

Let's propose that subjective space[4], that is, intrapsychic space, can account for this question of time and outside-time in the unconscious, if one connects it with the hypothesis according to which the unconscious conforms to a double topological structure, at the same time Mœbian and Borromean, as I will explain further on.

4. See: Bursztein, J.-G., *Sur l'espace subjectif*, Paris, Hermann, 2012.

II.

An interpretation in terms of space of what Freud calls "historical truth"

2.1 Hypothesis of the structure of the unconscious

What is the notion of historical truth in Freud, which emerged within the framework of his reflection on the paternal function in *The Man Moses and Monotheism?*[1] (In this notion Freud designates the activity of *original mnesic traces*, inaccessible, but which one can characterise by their traumatic effects. Freud notes that they conform to a sort of *repetitive compulsion* where a traumatic event is reiterating which can neither be discovered nor signified.

What is this trauma which is repeating? Freud gets a hold of the idea that traumatic repetition aims to appease the subject, caught by an unconscious guilt linked to the power of the death-wish against the father. The father is above all a signifier which designates the impossible fusion with the mother, an impossible perceived by the subject as a *lack* which does not

1. Freud, S. (1934-1938), *op. cit.*

cease to repeat itself by way of *trace-letters*, writing it in the structure as a *lack-in-having* (*manque-à-avoir*).

Since this want-to-have becomes too insupportable, the subject is forced to identify with an object, in a fantasy, object of a fundamental masochism which cancels the subject. Freud named 'death drive' this structural masochism (the death drive is realised as separation-function from any object).

In 1964, in the *Four Concepts*[2], Lacan takes up this problematic again and situates the death drive in the gap between the symbolic order of signifiers and the lack of *jouissance*. The death-wish directed at the father, as a wish to abolish the paternal reference, is therefore placed under the principle of repetition that Lacan designates as repetition-automatism, on using the Aristotelian category of *automaton*. Then he names *tuchè* the contingency of the lack-of-being (or want-to-be) which emerges from the fact of the impossibility of a return to fusion. If one follows this problematic, one grasps that two ways are then offered to the subject:

– In the way of masochism which consists in putting oneself as Me, in the place of the object, to suffer by way of a fundamental fantasy[3] substitutes the Freudian term "original" with that of *fundamental fantasy*), in order to make good the lack. In this way, it's a matter for the life-drive as jouissance of the big Other, (JO);

– In the way of desire, the object is no more imaginary and no longer that of a masochistic fantasy, but a signifier, bearer of symbolic value which is extracted from the object of the masochistic fantasy. There it's a matter of phallic jouissance, (JΦ). In this way the subject accedes to the pure death-drive[4]

---

2. Lacan, J., *The Seminar, Book XI, The Four Fundamental Concepts of Psycho-Analysis (1964)*, The Hogarth Press and the Institute of Psycho-Analysis, London, 1977, translated by Alan Sheridan.

3. Lacan substitutes the Freudian term, 'original' with that of fundamental fantasy.

4. In this sense, the signifier can be said to be mortifying.

in the positive sense since it introduces the subject to his desire by separating him from the imaginary masochistic object, and inducer of the imaginary jouissance of the big Other, (JO).

Freud had noted that the first memory traces call the subject ceaselessly to fusion. One must, nevertheless, distinguish the traces bearing the missing fusion, trace-letters, from the first signifiers hollowed out of jouissance, the (S1) (master signifiers): these are the signifiers that witness taking into account the symbolic Law of the father—who prohibits the mother's body, signifiers that the subject has extracted from the maternal discourse. These trace-letters conform to *lalangue*, that is, to the chaotic modality of incorporation of language transmitted by the mother, language reduced to bursts of jouissance, stripped of any signification, whether imaginary or symbolic. Because of this fact, the trace-letters continually induce[5] an *effect of existence* and an *effect of lack-in-having some jouissance*. The stakes in a psychoanalytical treatment consists in displacing the call to the missing fusion towards a symbolic identification which accepts the lack and transform it into the lack-in-having (frustration) into the lack-in-being (castration), repressing the imaginary identification with the object and the guilt that it engenders.

But it's only at the end of his difficult journey in 1938, in *The Man Moses and the Monotheist Religion,* that Freud found the means to think this unthinkable origin by subjective deployment, that is, the *wish to murder the father* in the forms of its denial. Freud situates this truth at the origin in order to say it is not really present in an event. He names this origin 'historical truth' in opposition to 'material truth', the

5. Lacan, J., *Le séminaire. Livre XIX, ... Ou pire: 1971-1972*, Paris, Seuil, 2011. "One which is in question in the S1 produces the subject, let's say the ideal point in the analysis, is opposite to what to what it's about in repetition, the One as One alone. It's the One whatever differences which exist, all the differences which exist and are worth each other, there is but one, it's the difference" [translated for this edition].

latter being referred to an event whose trace can be refund. Moreover, historical truth bearing witness to the past origin is therefore fundamentally a *perpetual present*, a *real* which does not cease to engender defences against guilt. Still, there where Freud tried to think structure in a developmental way, Lacanian psychoanalysis makes the hypothesis of its existence always already given.

Well, how to think the alternation between lack of objects (trauma) and finding of objects (fantasy)? *The topological approach to time and outside-time* of the unconscious can reply to this question. To situate this alternation of lack and finding of the object in the space of representation of the Borromean knot, one grasps that this alternation expresses the passage of the subjectivised, iterative, present time as a length of time-traces recalling traumatic moments of lack-in-having of *jouissance*. It's necessary to make a supplementary hypothesis concerning the alternation between traumatic moments of lack and moments of finding the object (imaginary or symbolic) by way of fantasy. This iterative alternation between traumatic moments and moments of finding objects in the fantasy must be conceived as *alternation between two subjective spaces* which is expressed as an on-going alternation between two modalities of the Borromean knot:

– A modality of the Borromean knot in three homeomorphic dimensions, potential space where the topological zone of the object (a) is only a hole (topological), situating the lack-in-being;

– A modality of the Borromean knot in three heterogeneous dimensions, real space, as perceived by the subject as Real, Symbolic, Imaginary; which implies that the topological zone of the object (a) is no longer just the space where the lack-in-being is situated, but it is also the zone where the masochistic object of the fantasy is situated or the intercurrent object of fantasies of desire.

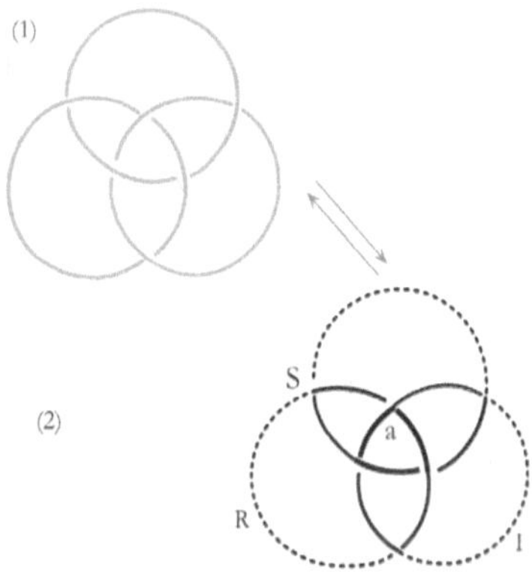

Figure 1: (1) knot of homeomorphic consistencies.
(2) knot of heterogeneous consistencies (R), (S), (I)

The dimensions in this knotting, are named Real, Symbolic, Imaginary and do not refer to the same *signifying density*, from that moment the dimensions will constitute a Borromean knot characterised by dimensions of heterogeneous space between them.

In the topological perspective which formulates the passage from the Freudian myth of the murder of the father (for example, Moses, Christ) to the structure, one insists on the fact that the assassinated father is resurrected in the form of a symbolic Law for the guilty sons.

I propose the hypothesis that this *unconscious symbolic Law*, making the dead father ek-sister, is nothing else than the symbolic phallus, Φ, signifier of the Law and of desire. I proceed at a crosswise pace between psychoanalysis and formalism (I define as crosswise the work of the psychoanalyst who succeeds in placing his unconscious thoughts in rapport with the objects of formalism). I situate this Φ in the place of the *point to infinity*, in the topological space underlying the structure. I am making this point to infinity the condition of *compactification* of the dimensions in the form of the consistencies (R), (S), (I) of the structure.

To resume the process of the epistemological passage from the myth of the dead father to structure, I am proposing that *the existence of the metaphor which is the symbolic phallus*, Φ, *expressing the iteration of the wish to murder the father*, (what Freud designates in terms of historical truth).

2.2 Point to infinity and the universe of transmitted language

In order to make this existence of structure like a whole, I identify *the infinite space of the universe of language*, transmitted by big the Other (the mother) with the subject, with a *half-plane of Poincaré*. In the subjective topology being put into place here, the *half-plane concept of Poincaré* expresses the space in which is situated *the universe of language* implicated by the existence of the subject-of-the-unconscious. Let it be noted that from this infinite set of the universe of transmitted language, the subject extracts a finite subset, namely the compacted straight line (in the case of neurosis). The said compacted straight line on which is situated the network finite in number of signifiers extracted from the elements of language, implicating, on the one hand, a fusional demand (that of the mother), on the other hand, the prohibition of fusion (the law of the symbolic father). This unconscious network constitutes the frontier of a closed consistency (Topologically, the interior of the circle constitutes what one can call a hole in space, that is to say a closed cut); it is linked to the potentiality of the symbolic phallus Φ, as well as to its actualisation into certain privileged signifiers (S1→S2). Let's consider that the *virtuality of the point to infinity* that I identify, by the way, with the function of the symbolic phallus, Φ, metaphor of the Name-of-the-Father[6] and signifier of desire, exist potentially

---

6. Lacan, J., *Concerning a discourse which would not be that of the semblant*, Book XVIII, 1971, Paris, Seuil, 2006.

on all the points of the compacted circle, and it is actualised in some few phallic signifiers which are inscribed on the edge of such a consistency by realising the unconscious network of the subject. In the case of the Borromean knot which inscribes the three dimensions (R), (S), (I) of subjectivity, the number of these consistencies is three.

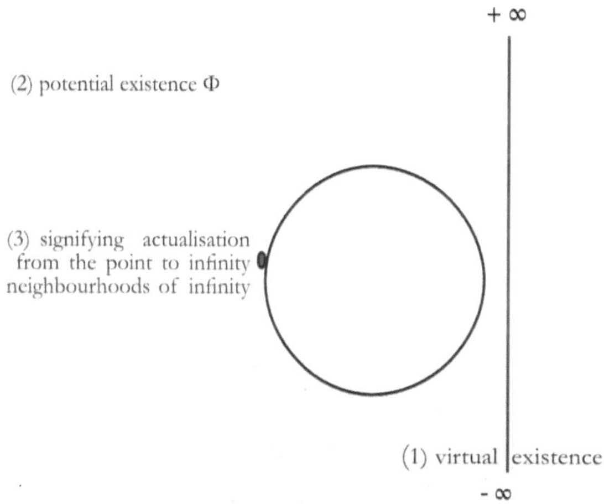

Figure 2: The existence of infinite neighborhoods

At (1) above, I am representing with this infinite straight line which divides the space in two, a cut space which induces a Poincaré half plane.

At (2) above, I am designating a Poincaré half plane as inscribing the neighbourhood with points to infinity. I attribute to these neighbourhoods with points to infinity the role of agents in the compactification of subjective space.

At (3) above, I identify this point-to-point signifying actualisation, potentially situated at any point of the homomorphic frontier with a Jordan curve.

III.

The question of time in Freud

3.1 The unresolved problem of time in Freud

No doubt, the problem of time in Freud stays as it was – also concerning its status and its modalities – *temporality lived as duration* and as *atemporality*. It also stays as it was in the way the primary character and fantasy of time are articulated in the structure of the unconscious with the secondary processes of the conscious, which are given as *diachronic time* in relation with the structure of the discourse that the conscious holds.

Starting with the problem of the dream and with the question of its representability, Freud perceived that the structure of the unconscious is at the same time prograde and retrograde. Although he doesn't schematise this point, he postulates the idea of a subjective space for the structure, making possible the appearance of dreams[1]. In *The Psychopathology of Everyday Life*[2], he shows that the unconscious is manifest in a series of formations: forgetting, errors, dreams, symptoms. From this perspective, he makes the hypothesis that habitual diachronic thought on time refers to the structure of conscious discourse. This is no longer the case in Lacanian psychoanalysis, where the approach to diachrony is referred to modalities of existence

1. Freud, S., A 'Metapsychological Supplement to the Theory of Dreams' (1917), *SE 14*, *op. cit.*

2. Freud, S., *The Psychopathology of Everyday Life* (1901), *op. cit.*

of the signifier, situated in the imaginary or in the symbolic. For Freud the progress of his theoretical conception obliges him to keep the level of the secondary process distinct, as it retains a logic of substitution between word-representations, that is to say, the elements of the signifier network, from what Freud calls *drive*, then the *id*. What differs from the signifier is the left-over that Lacanian psychoanalysis calls object (a). This object (a) is the left-over which has not passed to the signifier by way of language (signifying network) transmitted by the mother. It's necessary to face and resolve the difficulty which clings to a dimension of this object (a) which has not been conceptualised for Lacanian psychoanalysis as an energy or force, thinking which refers in Freud to the Galilean physics of the nineteenth century, but like an irreducible *differential movement*, generating the dynamic of the entire structure. This movement is nothing else but variations of the boundaries of the topological zone of the object (a) where the lack is inscribed as cause. Consequently, the Lacanian perspective marks itself off from all evolutionism in order to think the modalities of functioning of the unconscious in structural terms concerning spatial transformation (homeomorphism). So then, what Freud called *the sexual*, which he differentiated from biological sexuality, but he elaborated it within an evolutionist framework, using the categories of stages (oral, anal... is from now on conceptualised through the modalities, either of the fundamental fantasy or of its substitutes, that is, fantasies of desire. This is the reason that one can no longer refer psychoanalysis to whatever sexuality, for psychoanalysis collects modalities of *jouissance*.

Let's distinguish: *phallic jouissance* (JΦ) which is permitted, erotic or intellectual desire; the *jouissance of the big Other* (JO), prohibited, which puts the subject in a masochistic position by making him the object of the big Other; the *jouissance of Sense* which permits the subject to orient himself and to *jouir* the knowledge of his position, in the unconscious choice of *jouissance*; finally, the *jouissance* that Lacan calls *Other jouissance*, that of mnesic trace-letters which evoke lost presence, collecting *bodily jouissance marked by lack.*

How does one conceive the link and the difference between the signifying network and the object (a) at the centre of one and the same structure? The discovery-invention of the Borromean knot by Lacan around 1972 answers this theoretical and clinical question. Indeed, the Borromean knot, by virtue of its structure, allows the conceptualisation of the articulation at the centre of the same structure, the Borromean structure, of the network of signifiers situated on the frontier of the symbolic consistency, (S), with the object (a), situated in the topological zone of the frontier (R, S, I) as the following figure shows:

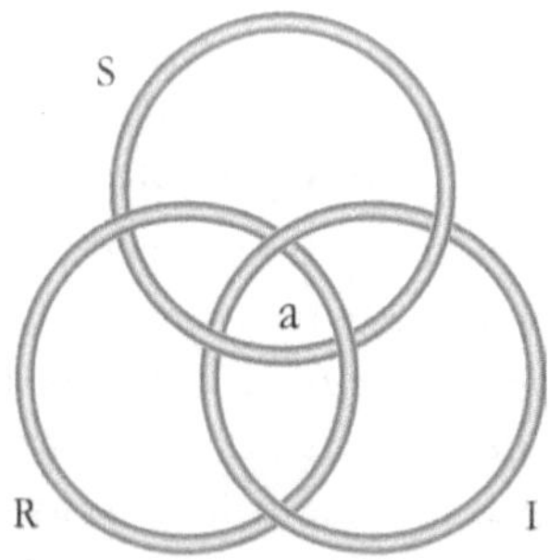

Figure 3: Standard Borromean Knot

On the basis of this topological separation, one grasps retrospectively why Freud, in his metapsychological researches of 1914, poses a differentiation between:

– The atemporality of the unconscious in the primary processes;

– The diachronic temporality of the secondary processes implicating the idea of time.

3.2 The atemporality of the unconscious

Recall that Freud had established that from his beginning the subject is confronted with questions which come to solicit his *unconscious theory of the world.* In effect, the existence of the structure induces the formation of an *unconscious theory of the world* for the subject where the latter poses himself questions on his origins and replies to it. It's in the article, 'Remembering, repeating and working-through' (1914g), that Freud formulates that repetition is a sort of *blind memory.* His concept of repetition-compulsion emphasises the permanence of repetition of the first traces of memory. Repetition without signification and without imaginary which affects the subject *in his Real.* This real of trace-letters is what constitutes the very foundation of the subject, its persistent trauma. That kind of *horizon of permanent presence always different from itself* is given as what one will call *duration.* On the contrary, the passage to the fundamental fantasy is inscribed through a signifying pair, (S1→S2) which forces to emerge, unlike the indefinitely differentiated continuity of traces of the repetition, what I will call instants-outside-time, that is, signifier moments are to be understood at the same time as limit-instants different from repetitive traces, as far as one grasps that the limits must not be inscribed on the different frontiers of the Real. This will be on the symbolic frontier. It is essential to grasp here that these *instants-outside-time* do not belong to time.

In *Introductory Lectures on Psychoanalysis* (1916-1917), Freud conceives that the positioning of the *sexual* only has its origins in the lack of jouissance of each subject. One result is the infantile experiences of the subject – *infantile sexuality* – but also another that Freud qualifies as 'pre-historic experience'. I identify this pre-historic experience which refers to a sort of inaccessible past, on the one had with the original demand of the big Other in its persistence, on the other hand with the reply that the subject gives to him, in his way to offer himself as object, through fantasy objects.

3.3 Beyond the pleasure principle

In 1920, in *Beyond the Pleasure Principle* Freud puts forward as the principle of subjectivity not so much as pleasure or unpleasure (the lack-in-having due to the absence of *jouissance*) but what he notices of structure. He discovers, in effect, that the liaison between the first memory-traces and the identifications with the first *parental images*. It is through the structure of three unconscious identifications that Freud thinks the internal transformations of structure.

1. Identification with the paternal images of the father and of the mother first *imagos*, constituting the original traces to which no access is possible. In this sense the latter are to be defined as the Real (of the subject);

2. Identification with certain traits of the father that Lacan calls unary traits as symbolic roots of the root of the Superego. For example, let's evoke the scatological traits of the rat man's father; these traits induce, in a superegoic fashion, a jouissance linked to excrement or to situations which metaphorises them;

3. An *imaginary*, hysterical identification with the craved for image.

3.4 Access to the difference between time experienced as duration and time experienced as succession of instances-outside-time

Modalities of unconscious thought that Freud calls primary processes ultimately refer to different times; it's about the unstable co-existence with two types of fantasies that concern the subject:

– The fundamental fantasy which refuses the lack in being linked to the perception of the absent penis on the body of the mother;

– The fantasy which, integrating this perception of a lack, induces a recurrent series of fantasies of desire.

Let's recall that the essential transformation of the fundamental fantasy picks up on the acceptance of castration by the subject. For the fundamental fantasy is propped up essentially by the dimension of the Imaginary, whilst the fantasies of desire are propped up by signifying occurrences linked to the dimension of the Symbolic, activated by the symbolic phallus Φ. There where Freud posits a primary process, it concerns the temporality of *traces of lack of jouissance,* in as much as the latter by their repetitive permanence are always differentiated. Let's then posit that the fantasy of desire, as thought process, including the perception of the lack (of penis), refers not to another modality of time, but to the route taken by (S1→S2) of the signifying chain. A route which induces *unconscious signification* for the subject, (note that the realisation of this pathway comes from the link that the subject establishes between the first two nominations, that of the mother and father) and which must as such be considered as an *instance-outside-time.* Let's situate (S1) and (S2); the (S1) are emptied of *jouissance,* the (S2) as signifiers coming from the big Other. The (S1) being signifiers emptied of *jouissance* are situated on the real frontier of the topological zone of the object (a), as repetitive trace-letters of the lack of jouissance which are situated on the real frontier of the topological zone of the object (a).

One conceives then how the trajectories (S1→S2) do not cease bringing *jouissance* to the (S1) by way of the (S2) signifiers taken from the field of the big Other. (S1→S2) constitutes a route situated on the symbolic frontier of the topological zone of the object (a). I call (S3) the representative signifiers that I situate on the imaginary frontier of the topological zone of the object (a)[3] which is shown in the following figure.

3. I owe the nomination of (S_3) to the psychoanalyst Michèle Canon.

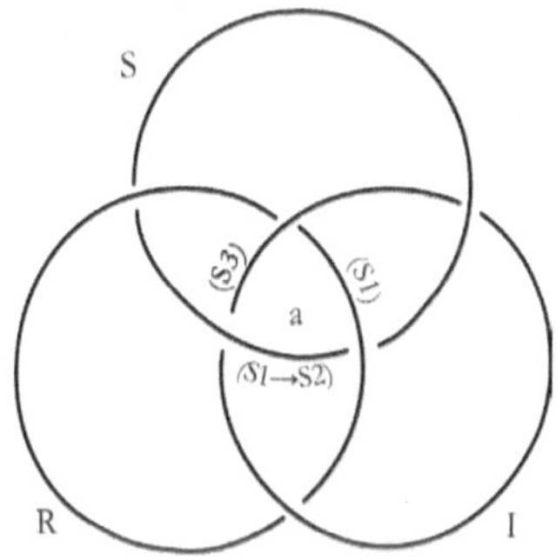

Figure 4: Situation of (S1), (S1→S2), (S3), on the frontiers of the topological zone of the object (a)

I am calling (S3) the capture in the imaginary by the signifying unity of the topological zone of the object (a) which emerge from the reading of the three frontiers of the object (a): it's the function of metaphor.

IV.

The unconscious, its Borromean structure (R, S, I)

4.1 The fact of the structure's existence

Let's firstly say that structure is always given as potentially constituted by all its elements. How do we conceive that? Let's start from the fact that there is for the subject always a *retroactive effect of language on itself.* Retroactive effect of language as an interaction between the pole of origins of the structure and its effects. It has to be admitted that the *signifier One* is nothing else but *the virtual element* of the structure constituted as a non-differentiated RSI knot, being deployed under the action of the symbolic phallus Φ, deployed as an (R, S, I) knot. This latter is a knot in which all the consistencies are named and differentiated.

Figure 5: Virtual knot

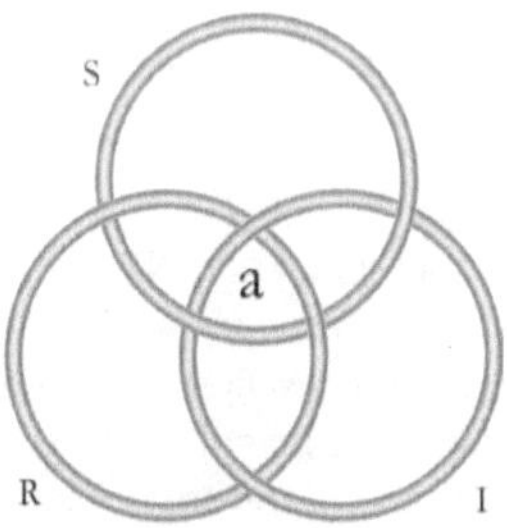

Figure 6: Realised knot

In the virtual knot one notes that the three dimensions (R), (S), (I), are potentially constituted as three homeomorphic curves. These curves do not become differentiated consistencies except by the unconscious designation of the subject who locates them, differentiates them in what will be theorised as (R), (S), (I). It's important to grasp that in the theory this structural deployment is substituted for what Lacan called the *myth of Freud.* In the category of the Oedipal myth Lacan designates the fact that Freud had a need to think the existence of the unconscious on the basis of the mythical element of the murder of the father and of the creation of the law to pacify the remorse of the filial assassins, installing actually the *symbolic Law.* It's what he calls the *myth of Oedipus*[1] In the thought of Freud it's the call for help of the hysteric which is imposed, the murder of the father being the substitute for the refused castration. Indeed instead of accepting castration the neurotic subject can do nothing other than to kill his father with intent in order to re-establish him in his function of Superego.

4.2 The concept of the real in psychoanalysis

It is nevertheless fundamental to differentiate the *real*[2] *of the subjective structure* (R, S, I) *from the real of the world and from the social real,* the subjective structure being plunged into a space separated by homeomorphic, Borromean consistencies where Jordan curves are separating the interior from the

---

1. Lacan, J., (2006 [1971] p. 173) The myth of Oedipus plays the role of *a knowledge claiming to be the truth.* In the structure extricated by the discourse of the psychoanalyst, knowledge (S2) *is put into a position of truth.* I am supporting myself on the remark of the mathematician Boas Erez in our Seminar "On the unconscious and time", Paris VII, 2016.

2. That's why one has to differentiate the subjective real (R, S, I) from the real of common sense and of the social real.

exterior which is demonstrated by the property of having no common point. I assign to subjective space the property of being closed by such consistencies. Such a property, that one shall designate as a closed cut, allows us to differentiate the subjective real from the real of the world. One must consider the Borromean knot as a knot between three closed consistencies which are homeomorphic to Jordan curves. In this way one can say that Borromean structure is the topos where subjectivity is situated. I differentiate the topos, topological space where the unconscious is situated, from places which are close to Euclidean space and to conscious rhetoric. There you'll find the difference between Lacanian topology and Freudian topography.

Moreover, one has to admit that these closed spaces are constituted by open topological sets, potentially having an infinite number of elements. The difficulty consists in thinking that this closed space is a space whose boundaries are excluded. This is the meaning of open topological sets. This topological property allows an introduction, in the closed space of the subjective, the signifiers which affect the subject. It's how nature separated from subjective space and its character of open topological sets allows one to think how subjectivity retaining such a topological property is a *protector space* (it's what some have tried to describe with the notion of ego-skin[3]). This topological property is missing in the case of autism[4].

This topological approach by way of subjective space allows one to argue that there exists a radical separation between the structures of individuals at the level of the social, individuals who are affected by the modifications of that social structure, and the subjective structure which retain the only topological spaces, irreducible to the space of the ambient world. It's an error of perspective to believe that psychoanalysts should

---

3. See: Anzieu, D., *Le Moi Peau*, Dunod, 1995.

4. See: Burgoyne, B., Autism and Topology, in *Drawing the Soul: schemas and models in psychoanalysis*, 2000, London, Karnac, 2003.

confront in their theory and practice what certain analysts call a 'new real', 'the real of the twenty-first century'. According to these psychoanalysts, the real would not depend uniquely on its space but would retain new social determinants, that which they assign to the couple capitalism and science.

4.3 Differences between repetitive time and atemporality of instances outside time

Rather than to attempt to establish an imaginary genealogy of the putting of structure into place, like Freud attempted brilliantly with the Oedipal complex and the myth of the murder of the father, the hypothesis of the existence of structure allows one to think the existence of the subject.

Let's recall that the symbolic phallus Φ is the metaphor in act of the Name-of-the-Father. In the topological structure of space, this Φ, *point to infinity*, is the pre-condition for the *compactification* of space not ceasing to generate the nodal structure in the form of a Borromean knot. The space of representation of the Borromean knot allows the analytical experience to be situated in the structure[5]. In the Borromean structure the Borromean knot is realised in the form of an iterative passage from *lack* to *fantasy* as the following figure indicates.

5. Lacan, J., *Book XVIII, D'un discours qui ne serait pas du semblant: 1971*, Paris, Seuil, 2006, p. 79.

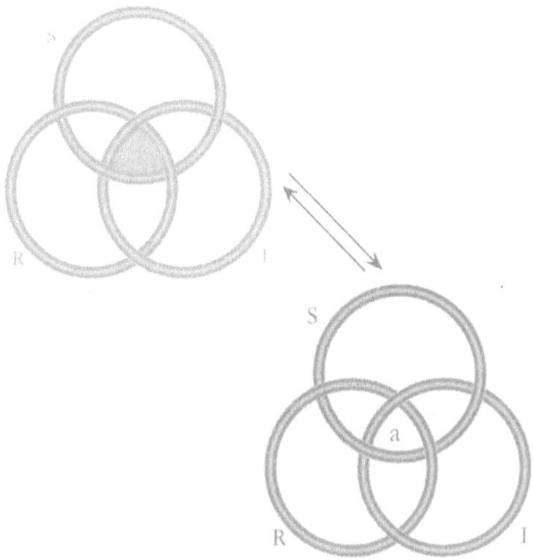

Figure 7: Iterative passage from lack to fantasy

The topological zone which does not cease to engender the modality (R, S, I) is referred to a topological hole in which I situate the lack. This lack is only the real where RSI is not deployed. It becomes the object (a) on deploying the topological zone (R, S, I) as a Borromean knot.

It's why the subject passes from its *invariant identity*, $\sqrt{-1}$, as the irreducible point of the want to be, to the variant identities (S1→S2), trajectories realising the fundamental fantasy under which the structure is subjectivised. (Let's note that this invariant identity, where <i>, the image of the body is equal to $\sqrt{-1}$ and witness to the irreducibility of the Imaginary to a real number.)

Let's identify *repetition* as aleatory movement of traces of affect in the real, to trace-letters marking the want to have of jouissance situated on the real edge of the frontier of the topological zone of the object (a). To show the difference, let's identify the *atemporality* of the unconscious with the inscription of the first signifying trajectories, (S1→S2) situated on the symbolic frontier of the topological zone of the object (a). Let's situate the (S1) non-linked to the (S2) on the real frontier of the topological zone of the object (a), besides, locus where the trace-letters are situated. Let's add that the imaginary frontier of the topological zone of the object (a) is the locus of potential representations which are the representative extracts of the signifying movement (S1→S2) in the unconscious, representations that we have called (S3).

Let's note that it's the inscription of the signifiers (S1→S2) on the symbolic frontier of the object (a) which causes this signifying inscription to escape *the pure repetitive and traumatic time* of trace-letters inscribing *the lack of jouissance.*

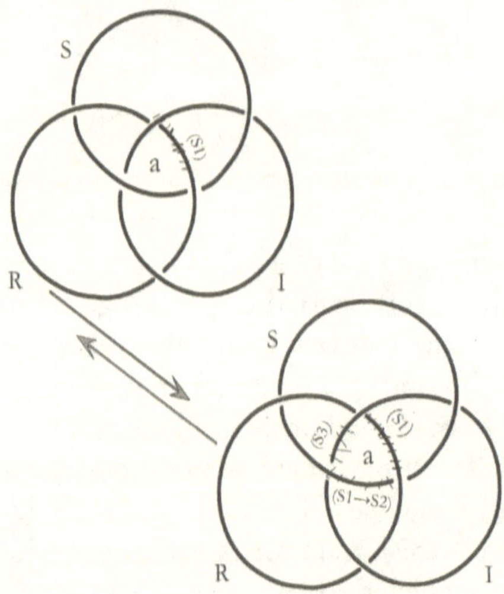

Figure 8: Iterative passage from trauma to fantasy

I name *instances-outside-time* this signifying inscription on the Symbolic. Let's note that the margins of the consistencies are *limits* separating at the same time the internal from the external and the consistencies between them. It's how the trajectory of (S1→S2) situated on the margin of the symbolic consistency can be said to be an atemporal unconscious, in so far as the fundamental fantasy does not cease to be rewritten in multiple scenarios. Whatever the signifiers are that express it, the incestuous-masochistic content of the fundamental fantasy remains always the same. In this sense, it's *about instances-outside-time, instances which do not belong to time*, which only apprehend themselves as always different moments, in opposition to *repetition* which does not cease making time appear as a *continuous potential*. It's what Bergson named duration (*durée*). In any case, different to Bergson, psychoanalysis allows a conception of modalities of time: modalities such as instances-outside-time and as those passing to the conscious.

This difference between the *present of repetition* and the *instances-outside-time* doesn't go without evoking what Aristotle set down in *Physics* IV[6] with respect to the fact that the instances-outside-time are like *limit instances*, not ceasing to divide time *between a before and after*. By virtue of repetition of traces, the *continuity* of a present is induced 'which does not cease not to be'. This Aristotelian, psychoanalytical interpretation allows one to grasp that for reason of the *function of limit*, the instance no longer belongs to time. From the psychoanalytical point of view, it's necessary to conceive *that these instances-outside-time are inscribed as trajectory between two signifiers* on the symbolic frontier of the topological zone of the object (a). This is why, different to Bergson[7], who accents duration (*durée*), due to the fact of spatialisation of time in the space of the Borromean knot, one grasps that *time is no longer just that of duration* induced by the continuity of traces constituting a *continuum*. Let's designate this *continuum* by the psychoanalytical category of *Real*, as divisible duration, as blind duration, that of the immediate, *which only exists by not being*, that is to say it exists only as *vanishing point*.

6. Aristotle, *Physics Book IV*.

7. See: Bergson, H., 'An Essay on the Immediate Data of Consciousness', Stanford Encyclopaedia of Philosophy, online.

V.

The difference between time and outside-time in the unconscious

5.1 Time in the conscious experience

The concept of unconscious, as one forgets it all too often, is not the contrary of the concept conscious, but it picks up a new hypothesis, that of thought as Mœbian structure situating the unconscious/conscious as a continuously iterative dynamic.

Freud, not having been able to develop this question, argued nevertheless that this unconscious/conscious works on a discontinuous, perceptive process. It was by way of the metaphor of the 'mystic writing pad'[1], (that he thought the inscription of traces (which he called traumatic) potentially inscribed and effaced in the psychical structure. He added that these discontinuous, perceptive traces, always active, erratic, referred to a sort of perpetually active present. But Lacan distinguishes the traces marked as emptied of *jouissance*, the (S1) are considered to be signifiers waiting for a signification coming from the field of the Other, that is to say, a signification coming from the (S2).

From this perspective the notion of time takes on several meanings:

---

1. Freud, S., 'A Note upon the Mystic Writing-Pad' (1925), SE 19, Hogarth Press and the Institute of Psychoanalysis, p. 227ff. This Wunderblock is translated into English as "mystic writing-pad" and into French as "le bloc magique".

It's at the same time the repetition of a present which is escaping and which only exists by not being[2], at the level of the real of the mark of letters, carriers of frustration and of lack, and of outside-time at the level of the first connections, at the level of the first connections between (S1) and (S2), that is, (S1→S2). These first signifying connections are constitutive of the fundamental fantasy.

5.2 The Freudian and Lacanian reformulation of the first theory of the psychical apparatus

In order to follow the passage of the Freudian theory to Lacanian psychoanalysis, one must note:

1. That the passage of a theory of the psychical apparatus centred on the drive concept to a conception of the psyche centred on the substitution of signifiers (dreams, errors, symptoms...) implies new hypotheses concerning the status of time.

2. In effect, *time is no longer conceived as a perpetual present, but as a repetition which finds its status in this topological perspective.* Lacanian psychoanalysis reformulates the concept of drive, always linked to a theory of force in a *causal theory of the object (a)*, linked to a conception of variations of subjective space. Here repetition designates the variations in the traces of the lack-in-having, trace-letters inscribed on the real frontier of the topological zone of the object (a). This latter only plays the role of the object-cause across the variations of the frontiers of its topological zone (R), (S), (I).

I am not treating here effects and reasons for this repetition when it passes neither to the signifying connections nor to the fantasy. Its effects are known; these are traumatic dreams, and passages to the act (impulsive acting out).

---

2. Lacan, J., *Le séminaire, Livre XVIII, D'un discours qui ne serait pas du semblant:* 1971, Paris, Seuil, 2006.

VI.

The modalities of outside-time in the structure (R, S, I)

6.1 Differences between trace-letters and first signifiers (S1)

From the perspective of the passage to a temporality other than the one of pure repetition, this time must therefore be conceived as an *outside-time*, that is to say as a succession of instances differentiated the ones from the others.

For Freud, this capacity of the psychical apparatus to realise itself in signifying liaisons is inseparable from his discovery of transference. In 1914, in 'Remembering, repeating and working-through'[1], he remarks that the transference is opposed to remembering which leaves the subject in the grip of *repetition*. In consequence, he assigns to the psychoanalyst the task of working with the analysand in order to support the return of memories and to surmount the repressions. It's only in 'Constructions in Analysis'[2] that he understands that one cannot lift *infantile amnesia* and therefore one cannot remember a past which does not exist, hence the idea of having

1. Freud, S., 'Remembering, Repeating and Working-Through (1914), *SE XII*, The Hogarth Press and Institute of Psychoanalysis, 1958, Vintage 2001.

2. Freud, S., 'Constructions in Analysis' (1937), *SE XXIII*, Vintage 2001

to substitute for this time that does not exist a *true fictive time*, that of the 'construction in analysis'.

It is Lacan, who, in the second period of his research in 1975, theorised the difference between trace-letters, inductive of the repetition of the lack of *jouissance* and signifiers (S1) emptied of *jouissance*. One has to conceive then of a theory other than that of the *subject of the unconscious*. This would be a theory of the *subject-of-speech*. This subject is the one that is constituted by *the trace-letters*[3] of the lack of jouissance emerging in lalangue. 'Lalangue' is language not emptied of jouissance, language without subject, without phallic organisation, opposite to what the first signifiers are, that is, (S1).

6.2 THE DEATH DRIVE IN THE FIRST SIGNIFYING CONNECTIONS (S1→S2)

At present, if one conceives that the death drive as beyond the pleasure principle is linked to the symbolic function of a separation from the object (for Freud) or from the imaginary relations of the object of the fantasy (Lacan), one grasps:

– how, in a first case, the subject is annulled in a masochistic way in <i>, his narcissistic image;

– or, how, in a second case, the subject can be relieved pf the imaginary aspect (-φ) of his narcissism, on condition of having passed to *intercurrent fantasies of desire*, instead of remaining cornered in his fundamental fantasy.

In effect, from 1924, in 'The Economic Problem of Masochism', Freud thinks that there exists a principle anterior to the *pleasure principle*, that is, the *death drive*. He then has to conceive of an original, connecting principle that I designate as the linkage of signifiers (S1→S2) which realises this death drive; admitting, then, that this first connection (S1→S2)

3. Already Aristotle named these indivisible sounds 'letters', *grammata* Poetics, 1456b23-24.

generates a separation from any possible object, and hence leaves the subject perpetually traumatised.

In psychoanalytical treatment one observes the existence of what Freud calls the *negative therapeutic experience.* The latter expresses the tendency to subjective annulment, in the absence of objects which are the support of any identification. In this situation, time is subjectivised as pure repetition of a perpetual present engendering the pain of existence due to the traumatic repetition of the *lack-in-having*. One can observe such an experience in autism (even if the latter is not afflicted by this sort of suffering) where the structure (R, S, I) is not deployed in three separate consistencies (R), (S), (I), shown in the following figure.

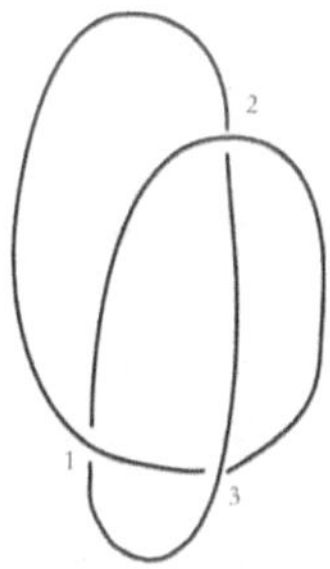

Figure 9: Structure of autism

6.3 The passage from the theory of the drive to that of the object (a)

If, for the post Freudians, the object is deployed like the passage of the prop object to the drive object, it is not at all the same in Lacanian psychoanalysis.[4] The latter reduces the concept of object by arguing that it's rather about a *function of*

4. Except, perhaps, for Laplanche, J., who proposes the concept of source-object in order to think the alternation of the trace-letters and of the object.

the object, function which is constituted across two modalities of the object (a): that of the *lack* and that of *support for the fantasy*. In fact, on the basis of the theory of the object (a), one grasps that the prop object of the post Freudians what they call *primary object* metaphorises a density sufficiently important of trace-letters capable of constituting the big Other as a fantasy-object. As for Freud, he theorises the genesis of the structure as the first moment of melancholy observed in the experience that he discusses in his article 'Mourning and Melancholia'[5]. In this text, he leaves on one side the question of non-access to the original object and clings to the couple, maternal presence and absence. He uses as example the joy and deception of his grandson whose game Freud observes with the reel, throwing it out of the cot uttering the phoneme '*o*'and pulling it back in again by the attached string uttering the phoneme '*a*'. Freud interpreted these phonemes as *fort/da,* gone/there, which represent his mother's movements as disappearance/return. Freud theorises this first object as potentially lost and potentially refund. Let's associate with the absence of the object (*fort*) lack of jouissance, frustration, and with the return of the presence of the object (*da*), jouissance. Moreover, let's note that what one calls the branding of the *subjective substance* by *jouissance* and its lack is expressed at the level of phonemes with the '*o*' of frustration and the '*a*' of satisfaction. I will use this term *substance jouissante,* which comes in the wake of Lacan's advances on *lalangue* and speech around 1975. This term is linked to the transformation of the concept subject, which is no longer uniquely the *pure barred effect of the signifying play,* but which becomes the subject-of-speech, divided in the types of his *jouissance.*

It's therefore in these trace-letters that is realised the succession of sequences: *object of lack/object of the fundamental fantasy.* Here it's the about the normal neurotic development of the structure, and not what happens in psychosis or in autism. It has

5. Freud, S., 'Mourning and Melancholia' (1915), *SE IV,* Vintage, 2001.

to be admitted that the object that is lacking and the object of the fantasy metaphorises the mother as a *total presence*. This total presence is the internal echo of the *lost Thing*. It's the repetition of these sequences which makes the objects of lack and fantasy alternate (what the post Freudians call 'passage to the object') which permits the subject to escape the traumatic neurosis as well as the *pure time of repetition*, a kind of perpetual present which is linked to it. Lacanian psychoanalysis goes beyond in its theory and its epistemology the notion of the couple drive/object which served Freud to think the deployment of the structure.

The sequence, where the modality of object (a) as lack and that of the object (a) as support of a fantasy alternate, are inscribed by series of alternations in an iterative way at the level of the Borromean knot where the unconscious is situated, as the following figure shows.

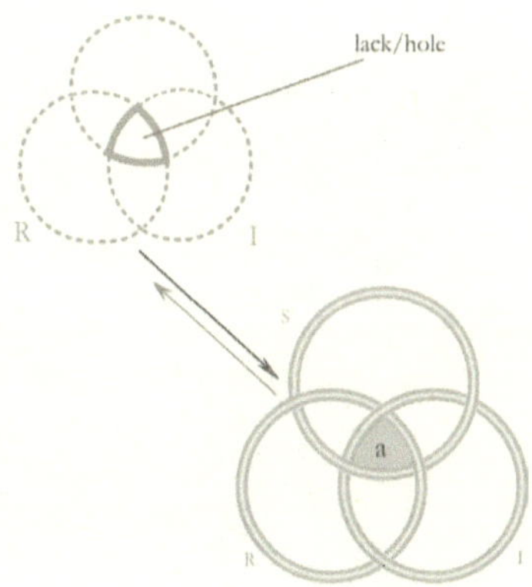

Figure 10: The modalities of the topological hole, lack/object (a)

VII.

Time and outside-time in the transference, the intervention of the psychoanalyst

7.1 Time of repetition and time of the fantasy

Freud did not thematise the conjunction between the impossibility of moving beyond the traumatic moment of the repetition of the trace-letters in relation to the hateful modality or absent modality of the big Other like the English psychoanalysts will do it, for instance Winnicott and Bion. Freud preoccupied himself especially with the connection between the repetition of the first trace-letters in their link with the object, what Lacanian psychoanalysis names the object (a) as the support of the fantasy. It is then in Lacanian psychoanalysis that the problem of temporality is made precise as temporality of the process of repetition, what I call the *time of the perpetual present*, experienced as *duration and inexistence* linked to and induced by the first trace-letters. In the same way I call *instances-outside-time* the temporality of signifier sequences (S1→S2) constitutive of the fundamental fantasy.

7.2 TRANSFERENCES AND DEPLOYMENT OF THE STRUCTURE (R, S, I)

The stake of the psychoanalytical work necessitates a grip on how the structure is deployed (R, S, I) what the post Freudians call the drive-object couple. It's then that one can say that this deployment articulates *the intrapsychic*, that is, the space (R, S, I), with the *intersubjective*, that is, the *original deal* which has become the first trace-letters and signifiers which come from the big Other.

The deployment of the structure (R, S, I) is realised in the space of the Borromean knot (except in certain forms of autism and psychosis), space in which the topological zone of the object (a) is, in that space where by means of the fantasy is realised the sudden appearance of what one calls the *objet.*

1. But contrary to the post Freudians who establish two categories, the drive and the object, psychoanalysis puts the accent on the fact that the object (a) is at the same time an active *causality* and an *object* constituted by its identification with the signifiers which play the role of imaginary or symbolic objects. (Take Freud's example in the Rat Man Case[1], the signifier complex, 'anus-rat' penetrating the anus, plays at the same time the role of a sadistic drive and that of object of the sadistic drive

2. Because of *hylomorphism*, characteristic of signifiers, the object can cease to be an element situated in the unconscious network, that is to say on the frontiers of the consistencies (R), (S), (I). It is then *realised* as an effect of *jouissance* in the three topological zones of jouissance, (JO), (JΦ), (JSense]. (Under the term 'hylomorphism', I designate the possibility for the signifier to have a potential existence or to be acting in real existence either as an element of unconscious sense or as an effect of *jouissance*.)

---

1. Freud, S., 1909d.

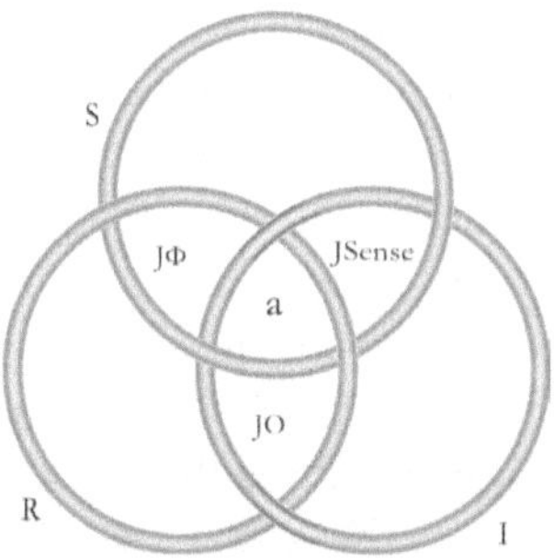

Figure 11: The topological zones of jouissance

7.3 The interventions of the psychoanalyst

In order to allow the analysand to escape the traumatic repetition, the psychoanalyst must, as Winnicott says, incarnate a sort of *transitional space*. In this perspective, one conceives that it's because the psychoanalyst is situated in the place of the symbolic phallus corresponding to the topos of the infinity point in the structure – that is to say, in the place of all the significations possible[2] – that he can incarnate for the analysand the place of the object (a) which causes desire. It's the reason for which the possibility[3] is opened for the subject to bring about the appearance of new signifiers (S2) which are substituted for those which are the mortifying of the first signifying connection (S1→S2), inducing repetition. It's why one defines the (S1), inaccessible as such, as it becomes evident in the treatment of the first unconscious representations (S2) under which the master-signifiers subjugate the subject to the will supposed omnipotent of the big Other.

2. See: Lacan, J., 'L'étourdit' 1972, in *Autres écrits*, Paris, Seuil, 2001.

3. This idea of possibility, or of possible, cannot be confused with what Leibniz calls 'essence'. The possibles depend, in order to be actualised, on the subject's choice.

The new signifying deal (S2), when it comes to be substituted for the first deal, represses the latter and induces the emergence of a fundamental fantasy around the object (a). For the normal-neurotic subject, the signifying movement confines the subject to repetition (repetition manifest, in the experience, in the acute moments of melancholy) but also in an alternating movement which allows the passage to another signifying deal, (S1→S2), letting the subject escape repetition.

The temporality of the unconscious here is, on the one hand, that of a *perpetual present which does not ek-sist*[4], since the instant of the present does not cease to flee, and, on the other hand, that of an *outside-time* which is inscribed like the passage of traces experienced in the symbolic dimension of the signifier.

4. This idea recalls Aristotle's thesis of time which I explain in Ch. IX.

VIII.

Time and outside-time in the analytical praxis, the question of the après-coup

8.1 The psychoanalytical act

I want right now to place the accent on the function of the psychoanalyst who in the analysis devotes himself to bringing signifiers to the analysand, with the aim that they provoke in him associations permitting potentially to obtain a glimpse of his fundamental fantasy. The psychoanalytical treatment is a summing up of being nothing more than a succession of such sequences, the aim being that at a given moment the analysand abandons his reliance on this fantasy substituting a *play of fantasies of desire*. He then identifies with his symptom and transforms his narcissistic image by renouncing the abject, erotic object which makes him oscillate between pretension and horror. (Please note (-φ), that fundamental operation on narcissism.)

But how can the psychoanalyst bring new signifiers to the analysand?

I am making here a topological hypothesis, according to which the psychoanalyst, in so far as he is also defined by his position at the infinity point in the structure, can grasp the set of statements by the analysand; then from that infinite set of statements, he can extract some of the signifiers which concern the unconscious desire of the analysand as much as the erotic desire linked to the imaginary phallus as to the desire linked to the symbolic phallus.

8.2 The psychoanalytical session

First of all, let's recall that in the Lacanian perspective the *end of treatment* does not come back so much to the question of a change in the analysand's identity than to the possibility which is offered him to have a glimpse of his *fundamental fantasy*, to grasp the double nature of the imaginary object which reveals itself: brilliant/abject. Only this sufficiently reiterated glimpse obliges the subject to abandon his identification with the object of this fantasy, in order to transfer his identification in the symbolic with the signifying play of the unconscious network.

I hold to the position of *psychoanalyst* for whom the essential point aims at the *interpretation of the Saying of the analysand*, on the basis of listening to his *signifiers*. That's the crucial point: it consists in knowing whether the psychoanalyst can or cannot, by virtue of his knowledge, *extract* the signifiers which open the analysand's unconscious. It's not about the *power* of the analyst but of his own knowledge. The other psychoanalysts have nothing to say about this act: 'the psychoanalyst is only authorised by himself.'[1]. In this problematic, what counts is the interpretative reach of *the cut in the analysand's Saying*. This can come from the enunciation of the psychoanalyst of a signifier with multiple meanings or of a scansion of the session which interrupts the analysand's discourse.

The experience of the treatment shows that such a scansion, because it plunges the analysand into the *outside-time of the*

1. Lacan, J., 'The Proposition of 9 October 1967.' in *Autres écrits*, Seuil, Paris, 2001, p. 243.

fantasy, has for effect the obliteration of the time of reality, (as it happens in mourning), which confers on the lived time of the session its strangeness.

8.3 The passage of trauma to desire in the treatment

In neurosis the subject does not cling to the signifiers of desire, but to failure which is expressed as a hysterical or obsessional position. Indeed, the unconscious conflict imposes itself on the subject in a way that the latter has to defend himself against the unconscious *jouissance* commanded by the fantasy. In this case the subject inhibits his action under *superegoic commands*; it's what I call the first series of (S2's). In consequence he remains confined in a mortifying liaison between the first traces emptied of jouissance, the (S1), and the first signifiers extracted from the field of the Other, the (S2). These first signifiers (S2) command the subject to cancel himself in a masochistic fashion or in a lethal one[2], as long as the subject remains submitted to the repetition of his *fundamental fantasy*.

It's only within the framework of the psychoanalytic transference that can emerge for the analysand a few new signifiers which are substituted for the first ones with traumatic effects. The new sequence of (S2) separates the subject from the *jouissance* of the imaginary object in the fantasy and places it on the pathway of desire supported by a succession of *fantasies of desire*. In this case the imaginary object dressing over the *lack* is repressed to the profit of a succession of objects articulated to the symbolic and phallic dimension of the new (S2) which emerge in the treatment. (This is why one must define strictly

---

2. See: Lacan, J., *The Seminar (1964), The Four Fundamental Concepts of Psychoanalysis, Book XI (1964),* The Hogarth Press and the Institute of Psychoanalysis, London, 1977.

the *praxis* of psychoanalysis as the iterative production of *interpretative cuts* until the moment the analysand takes hold of the knowledge thus produced and terminates his treatment.)

This subjective modification implies a concept that the subject passes in transit across a succession of Borromean knots. The passage of a first Borromean knot is then produced whose symbolic density is weak and imaginary density strong, towards another type of Borromean knot whose symbolic density is strong and imaginary density weak. This passage in transit operates at the level of the frontiers of the object (a). In the first neurotic configuration it's the imaginary frontier of the object which plays the role of agent in the action of (R), (S), (I) of the topological zone of the object (a). At the time of the passage to desire it's the symbolic frontier which plays the role of agent. It's then necessary to admit:

– Then all of a sudden the neurotic subject is realised in the case of a Borromean knot;

– That the destiny of the subject depends on the new actualisations appearing in the Borromean knot.

In the present case it's about the actualisation of the symbolic dimension, overcoming the imaginary dimension, as the following figures show.

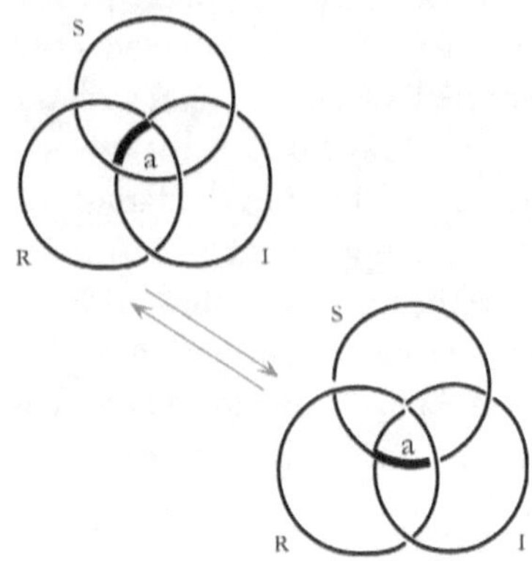

Figure 12: Variations on the frontier boundaries of the topological zone of the object (a)

IX.

The time-Symptom

If we now reflect on the Symptom as fourth consistency of the structure (R, S, I σ), we notice that it has a homogenising function of the different times and outside-times under which the unconscious is realised. If it is evident that the Symptom repeats and actualises the permanence of the first traces of lack of jouissance, the fantasy, as reply to the experience of lack, makes this present time pass, in its continuity, in its instances-outside-time, instances under which trace-letters are inscribed in the play of signifiers (S1→S2), in a succession of distinct moments. (It's on the basis of this succession of instances-outside-time that the subject imagines the time as constituted of a present which escapes from a past and present). The subject's access to symbolic castration permits it, ipso facto, to momentarily leave the space of the Symptom in order to re-establish the co-variance (R, S, I) of the structure.

This implies that the fourth consistency of the Symptom unties itself from the three others in order to double back mœbianly the consistency of the Real as the following figure shows.

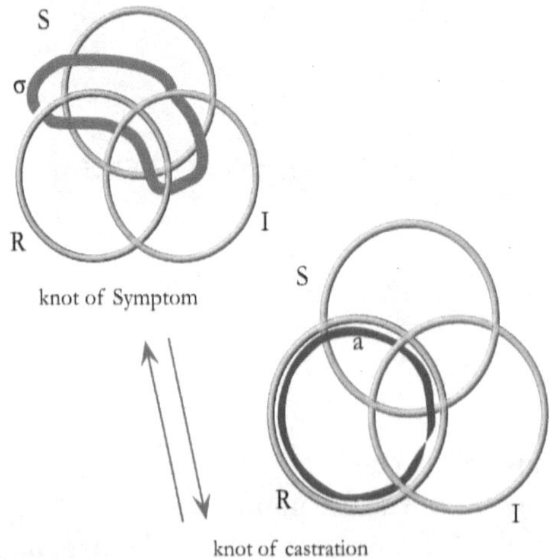

Figure 13: On the alternation between Symptom and castration

Nevertheless, one must not conceive this modification as definitive but as, on the contrary, incessantly renewed. Such a renewal of the transformation of the symptom has, besides, for effect to homogenise the *iterative Mœbianisation* of the structure and to pass onto what Freud called the *secondary process*. (This mœbianisation is the potential effect of the structure. Since Lacan, one knows that the structure of the unconscious implies at least two potentialities, the Mœbian, the other Borromean.)

These imply another modality of existence of time: the time of conscious diachrony, passing continuously from a past to a future, as the following figures show.

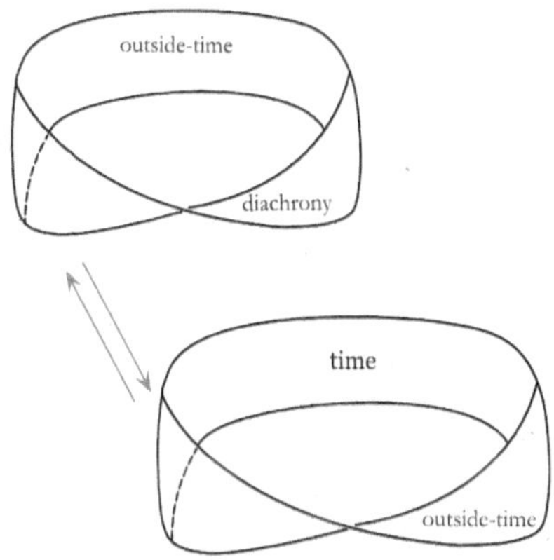

Figure 14: On the alternation between time/outside-time and diachrony

X.

The passage to conscious temporality

10.1 Passage to the diachrony of the conscious

Let's now take up the question of knowing how the two modalities of time of the unconscious, that of the present and that of outside-time, pass to the conscious, this passage always being linked to the structure of a *diachronic narrative.*

Basing ourselves on unconscious temporality that I have named *instances-outside-time,* constituted by the signifying liaison (S1→S2) inducer of a fantasy around the object (a), also inducer of a triplicate mode of *jouissance.*

Experience shows that in a recurrent way in the case of the structure's functioning, we pass in an incessant way from the unconscious mode of outside-time to the diachronic conscious mode. In order to explain such a possibility topologically, it's necessary to admit that there is a continuous *rotation of the topological zones of jouissance,* (JO), (JΦ), (Jsense), a rotation which covers and fills in for a moment the topological zone of the object (a). One must then conceive that *these three rotations realise the potentiality of the structure in the topological zone of the object (a), a Mœbius strip* putting (R, S, I) in a continuity. The structure (R, S, I) is the result of this Mœbius effect which permits the unconscious to pass to the signifiers and word-representations constitutive of conscious emergence. (For

Freud, the unconscious is not the opposite to the conscious but its other side. It concerns a new theory of thought divided between unconscious and conscious. From this perspective, it's wrong to say that there is no theory of the conscious in psychoanalysis.) This passage to conscious emergence is always realised in a diachronic fashion, that is to say, in the form of a succession in the mode of a before and after. Let's take up this question again of the passage of the unconscious to the conscious across the three following figures.

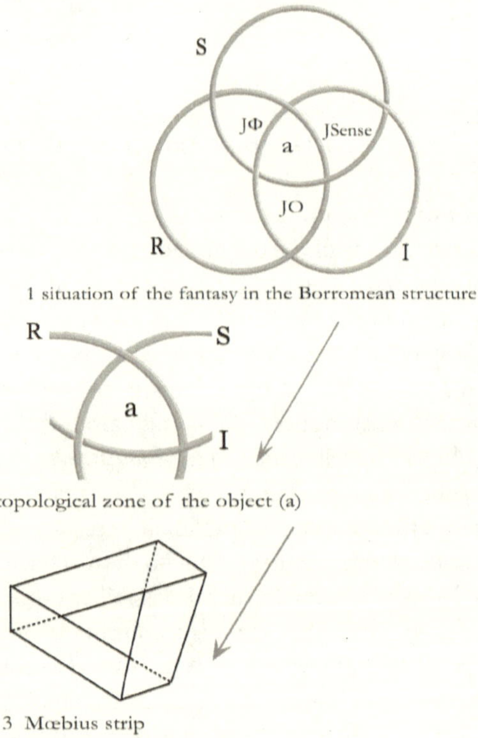

Figure 15: Passage to conscious temporality

This conception of subjective space I extract by transversality from Poincaré's theory of space-time, allowing me to think with the Borromean structure the relativity of space-time with language (R, S, I σ). The knowledge of the psychoanalyst takes up the liaison of space to time- what Poincaré called *group of transformations in space* – in order to think subjective space.

For the psychoanalyst the importance of Poincaré is how he knew to translate mathematically this relativity of space-time which he argued was about *objective time* as well as *subjective time.*

> We would not have been able to construct space, [...] if we did not have an instrument to measure it; of course this instrument on which we all take our bearings, the one we use instinctively, is our own body. It's by relations to our own body that we situate exterior objects, and the only spatial relations of these objects that might be able represent ourselves, there are their relations to our own body. It's our own body which serves us, so to speak, as a system of axes and co-ordinates.
>
> The space that I envisage in the preceding paragraph – and what I could call restricted space, was referred to axes of co-ordinates linked to my body; these axes were fixed, since my body wasn't moving and my members alone moved. What are the axes to which extended space naturally refer to, that is to say, the new space that I have just defined? We define a point by the outcome of the movements that it suits one to make in order to reach it from the basis of a certain initial position of the body. The axes are linked to that initial point of the body.
>
> But the position that I had initially perhaps arbitrarily chosen amongst all the positions that my body successively occupied. [...] if the memory more or less unconscious of these successive positions is necessary for the genesis of the notion of space, this memory can delve more or less far into the past. From there results in the very definition of space a certain indetermination which constitutes its relativity. There is no longer absolute space. There is only relative space with respect to a certain initial position of the body."[1]

1. Poincaré, H., in *Science et méthode*, éd. Kimé, 1999, pp. 93-94.

Nevertheless, different from what Poincaré proposes is the *knowledge of the psychoanalyst* which constitutes the system of 'axes of co-ordinates of one's own body.

In the following figure I am trying to show *how time as fourth dimension of space, noted here as t1, t2, t3*, varies in function according to the dimension of space it has to cross. I call 'little sigma', (σ) that fourth dimension of space.

One obtains a Borromean structure by the procedure of weaving the three dimensions (R), (S), (I); the figure allows the variations of time to be read according to variations of space in the Borromean knot.

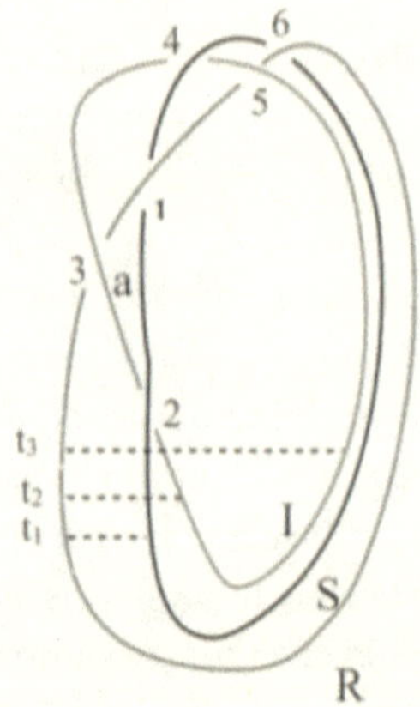

Figure 16: Time as fourth dimension of the structure (R, S, I σ)

10.2 THE UNCONSCIOUS AS POTENTIALITY OF MOEBIAN AND BORROMEAN STRUCTURES

To raise the question of the temporal status of the unconscious it has the character of a particular conception of time that I have called *outside-time* and at the same time an *ordinary temporality.* I have previously developed the hypothesis according to which the reference to the structure of the unconscious (R, S, I), topological structure implying potentially the existence of Mœbian and Borromean structures. Only this hypothesis on the potentiality of the structure takes account of this possibility of articulating the outside-time of the unconscious with *lived temporality*.

I'll start out this time with the standard presentation of the Borromean structure which expresses the structure (R, S, I) of the unconscious in the space of representation of a Borromean knot. I'll refer to this standard presented by Lacan. This Borromean knot has the advantage of being particularly readable in so far as it presents the topological zone of the object (a) at its centre. One can see on the following figure that this knot is constituted of seven subspaces, separated topologically from each other but in a constant interaction:

– 1: subspace of the object (a),

– 2, 3, 4: subspaces of the zones of *jouissance,*

– 5, 6, 7: subspaces of the zones of the subjective body (R, S, I).

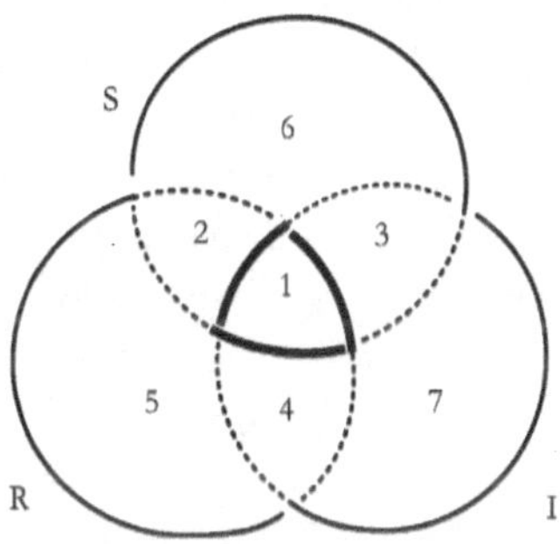

Figure 17: The seven sub-spaces of the Borromean knot

The question is then to know how this structure of the unconscious, thus presented in its Borromean form, is dynamised; how does its space start to move, and what's more, doesn't cease to be in movement. (Subjective space must be conceived as an ongoing iteration of spatial forms, the *spaces of representations* situating unconscious, signifying variations.)

I want to insist here on the fact that it's the iterative Mœbian[2] rotation of the three over and under, constituting the frontiers of the topological zone of the object (a), which generates the *cinematics* of the subjective space (R, S, I).

In order to conceptualise how this rotation of the frontiers of the object (a) can be produced, a hypothesis has to be made according to which it is realised under the constraint of the *lack*- that is, *privation, frustration, castration*- at the level of the imaginary object of the fantasy enrobing the object (a). It has to be grasped that this transformation rotates each frontier linked to the efficiency of the lack which implies a modification in the unconscious choice of the types of jouissance and, *ipso facto*, a modification of the subject's position in the modalities of his subjective body. By *subjective body*, I understand here the articulation of the *real body*, of the *symbolic body* and of the *imaginary body*, constituting subjectivity.

These transformations-modifications, affecting the *jouissance*, engender an infinitesimal incessant movement. It's like this that one can conceive how the Mœbian potentiality of the topological rotations of the frontiers of the object (a) dynamises in an incessant fashion the Borromean structure. The following figures permit one to grasp how the three homomorphic, topological subspaces present the subjective modalities with *bodyness* (*real body, symbolic body, imaginary body*) are solicited by the lack and are realised in the function of the modalities *of emptying the object of the fantasy* (frustration, privation, castration). In an iterative fashion, these modalities of lack induce, on the one hand, changes in the subjective position with respect to choice of *jouissance* modalities (jouissance of Sense, jouissance of the Other, phallic jouissance), on the other hand, changes of the localisation of the subject in his body: real, that is in his *real body*, in his *symbolic body*, in his *imaginary body*.

2. I am borrowing the hypothesis from the psychoanalyst and mathematician Jean Bourdiau who was the first to provide the solution to this problem.

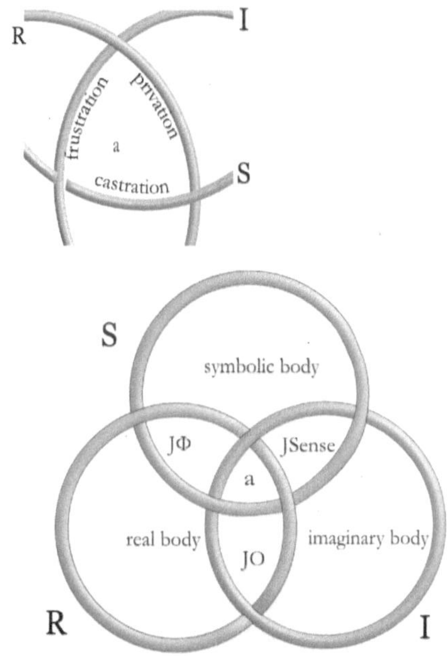

Figure 18: The interaction of the sub-spaces of the Borromean knot

In fact, in the frame of the Borromean knot's space these three over and under are represented here like a sort of *curvilinear topological triangle* which is assimilable to a triangle which can rotate on these three bases, (R), (S), (I). This rotation does not cease to be produced due to the fact of the separation between *jouissance* and signifiers, in the lap of incessant *bursts of lalangue*. These bursts of *lalangue* allow one to grasp what Lacan indicated in *Encore*): "[...] the unconscious is the fact that being, by speaking, enjoys, and I will add, 'wants to know nothing more about it." (Lacan, 1998 [1972-1973], p. 105). I will add that that means 'know nothing about it at all.' Language has to be characterised here like a structure of signifying elements, linked to the lexicon of words used by a community, having by this fact value of symbolic signification, differentiating it from *lalangue*- a term invented by Lacan. This term, lalangue, designates the elements linked to the *jouissance* transmitted by the mother. Let's note that the subject does not cease to constitute his singular signifying network until separation of the signifying elements from *jouissance*, what he doesn't cease to do by an iterative process of extraction apposite to the *principle of compaction.*

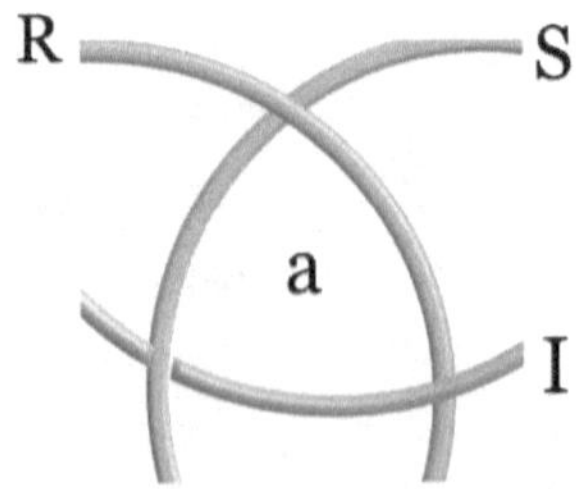

Figure 19: Curvilinear topological triangle of the topological zone of the object (a)

The presentation of the Borromean structure's dynamism allows one to apprehend how the outside-time of the unconscious is articulated to the lived temporality. For that, it has to be admitted that the time of the unconscious is nothing else than that of *instances-outside-time*. Under this concept of 'instances-outside-time', I designate the inscription of the temporality of internal transformations, emerging in the form of signifying elements on the frontier of each Borromean consistency. It's in that iterative fashion and continues that these instances-outside-time (not all, in function of the censorship) which number and transcribe all the internal transformations are continually rotated Mœbianly, in lived temporality in the conscious of the subject.

My argument is that in this problematic *the Mœbian-Borromean potentialities* are structural properties of the unconscious which in as much as cannot be situated in the spaces of representation under which this structure can be approached.

XI.

The topological foundations of subjective space

11.1 On the space of a half-plane Poincaré

In order to conclude this study, let's try for now to get a hold of what type of space and topological structure go back to the existence of Mœbian and Borromean spaces. It's necessary to return to the space that one calls *space of Poincaré*.

From the point of view of my subjective topology, I note that the *half-plane of Poincaré* is not what one might expect it to be, namely an actual half of a plane. It is not a question here of a metric reduction, but of a *potential space*, co-extensive with an *open cut* in space. One can conceive then that this half-plane Poincaré is a *space-quotient* which, from the point of view of psychoanalysis, does not cease to be realised as a plunge into the Mœbian spaces (unilateral).

11.2 An interpretation of the space Poincaré

Under the concept *bretzel structure* I have extracted the breakthroughs made by Lacan which go back to *holed spaces*. I designate at the level of what one can call the foundations, a topological structure susceptible of expressing the fundamental properties of subjective space, of its cinematic and temporal status as well as the outside-time of the unconscious.

1) The argument is that the infinite of subjective space is situated potentially in the *holes* co-extensive with all the signifying points of the space in the *bretzel structure*[1]. By these holes is expressed the *density of the One*, a density which is expressed by the causality of the object (a), in the form of an active lack, when this holed space is plunged into the structure of unilateral Mœbian spaces, in the form of closed surfaces.

2) Let's also take up the argument that the *continuity of subjective space* is potentially situated at any holed point of spaces generated by this bretzel structure, *the unconscious* is characterised therefore *as relevant to cuts outside-time* (situated in these holes, what I shall define as the signifying movement (S1→S2) *and as time*[2] (situated in the non-holed structure in space which I identify with the divided subject, $\mathcal{S}$).

This bretzel structure holed-not holed is represented as inscribing in the unilateral spaces in the form of Mœbian structures, the last being realised in the form of Mœbian strips with three half twists. I am making the hypothesis that these Mœbian structures are operators which in the Borromean structure of the unconscious allow the homogenisation of the fourth dimension of time with space. The three half twist noted 1, 2, 3 on the following figure the way by which the signifying instances-outside-time are articulated with the time of repetition.

1. I'll leave open the problem concerning the topological concept of the bretzel structure.

2. See; Lacan, J., *Topology and Time*, unpublished seminar.

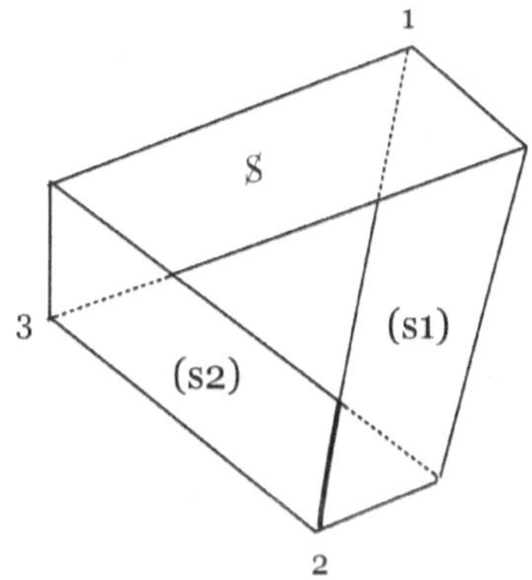

Figure 20: A topological articulation of the time of repetition of the instances outside-time and on the passage to conscious time

On this three semi-twisted Mœbius strip I situate the signifying instances-outside-time and simultaneously the times experienced generated by the third half-twist. It's to be understood that the mobility of the *signifying instances outside-time* is what I refer to the signifying movement (S1→S2) which is articulated to the times noted here $. This $ is nothing else than the divided subject as continuity infinitely differentiated from lived times.

The psychoanalysis here is not without the theory of Aristotle who distinguished the instances-outside-time as mobile, *ho pote on*, not without the theory of the subject, *hupokeimeinon*, as support from experienced times, what I shall define psychoanalytically as relevant to the Real. Everything happens as if the infinity of lived moments (time) are marked by a real which can only be inscribed as instances-outside-time as signifying movement (S1→S2) implicating Symbolic and Imaginary.

11.3 Space-time of the unconscious

Starting out from the hypothesis according to which the unconscious is co-extensive with the structure (R, S, I), I place the accent on the active difference between the Borromean structure and its spaces of representation- the Borromean knots—which realise the structure. I then assign to the three consistencies (R), (S), (I) of the Borromean knot, augmented by the fourth consistency of the Symptom/sinthome, the *structure of space-time of the unconscious.* The fourth consistency of the Symptom makes the variations of the three dimensions of space around the fourth spatial consistency conspicuous, which expresses the spatiality of the temporal dimension.

I insist here on the Lacanian nomination of the Borromean knot. Nomination takes account of the fact that the subjective structure is only realised on the condition that the dimensions of space are produced in a *space of representation.* The difficulty here consists in grasping that the spaces of representation are at the same time subjective and objective: *subjective* because they are forms of interpretation by the subject in the structure, objective because they are the spaces which finalise the existence of the subject's structure of the unconscious.

11.4 The psychoanalytical concept of time

On concluding this study on time, I will propose now a psychoanalytical concept of time. (I am nevertheless aware that it would be necessary to develop the preliminaries to such a presentation, all the more since I haven't done it. This task will be put off till later with the hope that others will get down to it.

I define therefore the psychoanalytical concept of time whose essence is found in space which has to be conceived of as *space of a cut, cut in space*. Moreover, one has to think that these holed spaces are realised in subjectivity as Mœbian structures. The latter represent the temporal dimension as *fourth dimension* inherent *in subjective space* as extension. (Different from the three other consistencies (R), (S), (I), I am not making from time a consistency but a fourth dimension of space, present in the structure as topos of the Symptom. The difficulty is to grasp that time, as fourth dimension of space, is realised as consistency of the Symptom in the structure.)

This relation between space and extension poses, in the lap of space, the irreducibility Poincaré (1999 [1908], pp. 93-94) of the Imaginary to which the theory of general relativity is witness.

References

ARISTOTLE. (2008). *Physics* I, 7, III, 207b, 34-208a4. New York, NY: Oxford University Press.

ARISTOTLE. (1975). *Categories* IV, I b2. New York, NY: Oxford University Press.

ARISTOTLE. (2013). *Poetics*. 145 6b 23-24. New York, NY: Oxford University Press.

FREUD, Sigmund. Notes upon a case of obsessional neurosis. In: *Two Case Histories. S. E., 10,* 1909d. p. 151-251. London: Hogarth.

FREUD, S. In: *Les premiers psychanalystes.* 8 Novembre 1911, Collectif, Minutes de la Société psychanalytique de Vienne, tome III: 1910-1911, Collection Connaissance de l'Inconscient, Série La Psychanalyse dans son histoire, Gallimard, 1979, p. 300. (trans: *Minutes of the Vienna Psychoanalytic Society. 3:1910-1911.* Herman Nunberg (Editor). New York: International Universities Press (p. 367).

FREUD, S. Remembering, repeating and working through. In: *The Case of Schreber. Further Recommendations on the Technique of Psycho-Analysis II. S.E. 12,* 1914g. (p. 122-145). London: Hogarth.

FREUD, S. *Introductory Lectures on Psycho – Analysis. S. E. 15-16* (1916-1917). Revised ed., New York, 1966; London, 1971.

FREUD, S. A metapsychological supplement to the theory of dreams 1915. In: *On the History of the Psycho – Analytic Movement, Papers on Metapsychology and Other Works. S.E., 14,* 1917d. (p. 217-235). London: Hogarth.

FREUD. S. Mourning and melancholia. 1915. In: *On the History of the Psycho – Analytic Movement, Papers on Metapsychology and Other Works. S. E., 14,* 1917e. (p. 237-258). London: Hogarth.

FREUD, S. A note upon the 'mystic writing – pad' 1924. In: *The Ego and the Id and Other Works. S. E., 19,* (pp. 225-232). 1925a London: Hogarth.

FREUD, S. Constructions in analysis. In: *Moses and Monotheism, An Outline of Psycho – Analysis and Other Works. S.E., 23*, 1937. (p. 255-270). London: Hogarth.

FREUD, S. *Moses and Monotheism.* 1938, *An Outline of Psycho – Analysis and Other Works. S.E., 23*, 1940a. (pp. 139-208). London: Hogarth.

FREUD, S. *The Psychopathology of Everyday Life. S.E., 6*, 1901b. (p. 1-291). London: Hogarth.

LACAN, Jacques. The Proposition of 9 October 1967. In: *Autres écrits*. Paris: Seuil. 2001.

LACAN, J. L'étourdit. 1972. In: *Autres écrits*, Paris, Seuil, 2001.

LACAN, J. *The Four Fundamental Concepts of Psychoanalysis.* 1964, *Book XI.* J.-A. Miller (ed.). B. Fink. (Trans.). (p. 304). New York: W. W. Norton. 1973.

LACAN, J. *The Seminar, Book XVIII, On a discourse that would not be that of the semblant.* 1971. Paris: Seuil. 2006.

LACAN, J. *The Seminar, Book XIX, …Ou pire.* 1971-1972. Paris: Seuil. 2011.

LACAN, J. *The Seminar, Book XX, Encore,* 1972-1973, translated by Bruce Fink, W. W. Norton & Co. New York and London, 1998.

LACAN, J. *The Seminar, Book XXIII, Le sinthome.* 1975-1976. Paris: Seuil. 2005.

LACAN, J. *La topologie et le temps, Topology and Time,* 1978-1979. Unpublished.

***

ANZIEU, Didier. *The skin ego.* New Haven, CT: Yale University Press, 1989.

ANZIEU, D. *Le Moi Peau.* Dunod. 1995.

BERGSON. Henri. *Time and Free Will: An Essay on the Immediate Data of Consciousness,* 1889; Dover Publications. Mineola New York. 2001.

BURGOYNE, Bernard. Autism and Topology, 2000, in *Drawing the Soul: Schemas and Models in Psychoanalysis.* London: Karnac. 2003.

BURSZTEIN, Jean-Gérard. *Sur l'espace subjectif,* Paris: Hermann. 2012.

LAPLANCHE, J. *Nouveaux fondements pour la psychanalyse.* Paris: PUF. 1984.

LAPLANCHE, Jean. *New Foundations for Psychoanalysis.* Translated by David Macey. Basil Blackwell. 1989.

NEWTON. *The Mathematical Principles of Natural Philosophy.* 1697.

POINCARÉ, Henri. *Science et Méthode.* Paris: Kimé. 1999.

POINCARÉ, H. *Last Thoughts*, http://hlombardi.free.fr/PoincaréDernièresPensée.pdf, consulted 26 June 2015.

Index of names

Index

Index of psychoanalytic notations

Index of formal concepts

Index of Aristotelian categories

Table of figures

Table of Contents

***

By the same author

2004 *Le renouveau de la psychanalyse dans l'hypothese borroméenne*, NEF.

2006 *Psychose et Structure*, NEF.

2006 *Vers une mathématique de l'inconscient*, NEF.

2007 *Névrose, nœud borroméen, espace de Hilbert*, NEF.

2007 *La structure mœbienne de la bisexualité*, NEF.

2008 *Jouissance féminine et hypothèse mathématique du continu*, NEF.

2009 *Une introduction a la science psychanalytique*, Hermann.

2010 *Nazisme et Shoah, une approche psychanalytique*, Hermann.

2010 *Expérience antique du salut et psychanalyse. Sur Yonah/Jonas*, Hermann.

2012 *Différence entre psychanalyse et psychothérapies*, Hermann.

2012 *Sur l'espace subjectif*, Hermann.

2014 *L'Ecclésiaste Une approche psychanalytique*, Hermann.

2015 *La différence homme/femme dans la sexuation*, Hermann.

2015 *Un commentaire psychanalytique de la Bible hébraïque*, Hermann.

2017 *L'inconscient, son espace-temps. Aristote, Lacan, Poincaré*, Hermann.

2017 *Cohérence philosophique de la psychanalyse. Aristote, Lacan*, Hermann.

2017 *Un lexique de topologie subjective*, Hermann.

2019 *Psychanalyse et philosophie borroméenne*, Hermann.

2019 *Philosophie de la Bible hébraïque et psychanalyse. Un lexique*, Hermann.

English

2008 *On the Difference between Psychoanalysis and Psychotherapy*, NEF.

2015 *The Topological Transformation of Freud's Theory*, London, Karnac Books Ltd.

2019 *Subjective Topology. A Lexicon*, Hermann.

2019 *My Lexicon of Psychoanalysis*, Hermann.

2019 *The Unconscious, its Space-Time. Aristotle, Lacan, Pöincaré*, Hermann.

German

2007 *Die Struktur der Andersheit Mann-Frau*, Turia & Kant, Wien.

2009 *Antike hebräische Heilerfahrung und Psychoanalyse. Das Buch Jonah*, Turia & Kant, Wien.

2012 *Die Psychoanalyse – eine paradoxe Wissenschaft*, Turia & Kant, Wien.

Hebrew

2004 *Ha-psychoanalysah Chel ha natzizm*, Resling, Israel.

2013 *Parchanout lacanianit al sepher Yonah*, Resling, Israel.

2017 *Parashot ha chavoua beri ha-psychoanalysah*, Idra, Israel.

Chinese

2018 精神分析科学 *(Jīngshén fēnxī kēxué)*, 北京师范大学出版社 (Běijīng shīfan daxue chūbǎn she, Beijing Normal University Press Group/Society Co).

Acknowledgements

I would like to thank Mr. Jean Bourdiau, psychoanalyst and mathematician, for the exchanges we've had with regards to this work. I thank Mrs. Michèle Canon, psychoanalyst, for the exchanges which allowed me to refine some of my hypotheses. I would like to thank Mr. Richard Klein for his translation. I also thank Mrs. Anne-Marie Lelong for her help.

www.ingramcontent.com/pod-product-compliance
Lightning Source LLC
LaVergne TN
LVHW090329210926
848480LV00004B/1349
* 9 7 9 1 0 3 7 0 0 3 1 0 2 *